Golden Opportunities: The Beginner's Guide to Trading Precious Metals

Table of Contents

Disclaimer

This educational material does not constitute a recommendation or opinion that an investment in certain financial products is appropriate for you, nor does it take into account your investment objectives, financial situation nor particular needs.

Before investing in any financial products, you must consider your objectives, financial situation and needs. Before you make any decision about acquiring a financial product, you should obtain and consider the relevant product disclosure statement. It is always recommended to use an independent advisor.

What are Precious Metals?

Precious metals are rare, naturally occurring metallic chemical elements that have a high economic value due to their scarcity, utility, and unique properties. They have been sought after and used as a store of value, an investment vehicle, and for various industrial and technological applications throughout human history. Some of the most well-known precious metals include gold, silver, platinum, and palladium.

Gold (Au): Gold is one of the most recognizable and widely traded precious metals. It has been used as a form of currency, a store of value, and in jewelry since ancient times. Gold is known for its malleability, ductility, resistance to corrosion, and ability to conduct both heat and electricity. These properties make gold valuable for various industrial applications, such as electronics, dentistry, and aerospace. In addition, gold is often used as a hedge against inflation and economic uncertainty.

Silver (Ag): Silver is another widely recognized and traded precious metal. Like gold, silver has been used as a form of currency, a store of value, and in jewellery for centuries. Silver is more abundant than gold, making it more affordable for investors and collectors. Silver has numerous industrial applications due to its high electrical conductivity, reflectivity, and resistance to corrosion. It is used in electronics, solar panels, photography, and various other industries.

Platinum (Pt): Platinum is a dense, malleable, and ductile metal with a silvery-white appearance. It is rarer than gold and silver, making it one of the most valuable precious metals. Platinum is known for its high melting point, corrosion resistance, and catalytic properties. These attributes make it particularly useful in the automotive industry for catalytic converters, as well as in jewellery, electronics, and chemical industries.

Palladium (Pd): Palladium is another rare precious metal with a silvery-white appearance. It is part of the platinum group metals (PGMs) and shares many of the same properties as platinum. Palladium is primarily used in catalytic converters for the automotive industry due to its ability to reduce harmful emissions. Additionally, palladium is used in electronics, dentistry, and jewellery.

The value of precious metals is determined by factors such as their rarity, utility, and the demand for their industrial applications. The prices of precious metals can be influenced by macroeconomic factors, geopolitical events, and changes in investment demand.

Understanding these factors and their impact on precious metals prices is essential for anyone interested in trading or investing in this market.

Importance of Precious Metals in the Global Economy

Precious metals play a significant role in the global economy due to their unique properties, scarcity, and varied applications. They serve as a store of value, a means of investment, and are used in numerous industries. The following points highlight the importance of precious metals in the global economy:

Store of value and hedge against uncertainty

Precious metals, particularly gold, have been regarded as a store of value and a hedge against economic uncertainties for centuries. Investors often turn to gold during times of inflation, currency devaluation, or geopolitical tensions, as it is considered a safe-haven asset. This helps maintain stability in the financial markets and ensures that wealth can be preserved during turbulent times.

Investment and portfolio diversification

Precious metals offer investors an opportunity to diversify their portfolios, reducing the overall risk associated with their investments. They often have a low correlation with traditional assets, such as stocks and bonds, which can help balance investment returns during market fluctuations. Precious metals can be invested in various forms, including physical bullion, exchange-traded funds (ETFs), futures contracts, and mining stocks.

Industrial applications

Precious metals have a wide range of industrial applications due to their unique properties. Gold and silver are used in electronics, dentistry, and aerospace, while platinum and palladium are essential components in catalytic converters for the automotive industry.

These metals are also used in other sectors, such as renewable energy, chemical production, and medical devices, contributing to technological advancements and global economic growth.

Impact on currency markets

Precious metals, especially gold, can influence currency markets. Central banks often hold gold reserves to back their currencies and maintain financial stability. Changes in gold prices and demand can affect exchange rates and the value of currencies, impacting international trade and investments.

Job creation and economic development

The precious metals industry, including mining, refining, and trading, contributes to job creation and economic development in many countries. The sector also supports various other industries, such as transportation, construction, and manufacturing, which rely on the supply of precious metals for their operations.

Overview of the Precious Metals Market

The precious metals market is a global marketplace where various forms of precious metals, such as gold, silver, platinum, and palladium, are traded. This market attracts a diverse range of participants, including individual investors, institutional investors, central banks, mining companies, and industrial consumers. The precious metals market can be segmented into different categories based on the form of the metal, the type of transaction, and the market participants involved.

When trading precious metals, it's essential to understand the different markets available and the characteristics of each. The three primary markets for trading precious metals are the spot market, the futures market, and the options market. Here's an overview of these markets and their key features:

Here's an overview of the precious metals market:

Physical market: The physical market involves the trading of tangible precious metal products, such as bars, coins, and jewellery. Transactions in the physical market can occur between individual buyers and sellers or through dealers, who act as intermediaries between market participants. The physical market is often characterised by localised pricing and can be influenced by factors such as supply and demand, geopolitical events, and changes in consumer preferences.

Financial market: The financial market for precious metals encompasses various financial instruments, such as exchange-traded funds (ETFs), futures contracts, options, and shares of mining companies. These instruments enable market participants to gain exposure to the price movements of precious metals without the need for physical possession. The financial market is typically more liquid than the physical market and offers a wider range of investment options.

Spot market: The spot market is where precious metals are traded for immediate delivery. Transactions in the spot market are typically settled within two business days. The spot market is highly liquid, and the prices quoted for precious metals represent their current market value. These prices serve as a reference point for other types of transactions, such as futures contracts and options. The spot market allows market participants to take advantage of short-term price movements and capitalise on opportunities arising from macroeconomic factors, supply and demand dynamics, and geopolitical events.

Futures market: The futures market involves trading standardised contracts that represent an agreement to buy or sell a specific quantity of a precious metal at a predetermined price on a future date. Futures contracts are traded on regulated exchanges, such as the COMEX division of the CME Group. The futures market provides market participants with the ability to hedge against price fluctuations, speculate on future price movements, or arbitrage price differences between markets. Some of the key advantages of trading precious metals futures include high liquidity, transparent pricing, and the use of leverage to control larger positions with a smaller initial investment.

Options market: The options market allows traders and investors to trade contracts that grant the right, but not the obligation, to buy or sell a specific quantity of a precious metal at a predetermined price on or before a specific date. There are two types of options: call options, which give the holder the right to buy the underlying asset, and put options, which give the holder the right to sell the underlying asset. Options can be used for hedging, speculating, or generating additional income in a portfolio. They are traded on regulated exchanges and over-the-counter (OTC) markets. Trading options on precious metals provides market participants with the flexibility to create customised strategies based on their market outlook and risk tolerance.

Mining stocks: Shares of mining companies offer investors indirect exposure to precious metals by investing in companies involved in the exploration, extraction, refining, and sale of these metals. The performance of mining stocks is influenced by factors such as metal prices, operational efficiency, geopolitical risks, and environmental regulations.

Understanding the differences between the spot, futures, stocks and options markets is essential for traders and investors looking to trade precious metals effectively. Each market offers unique opportunities and challenges, and selecting the appropriate market based on one's objectives, risk tolerance, and trading style can greatly impact the overall success of a trading strategy.

Trading Platforms and Brokers

Trading platforms and brokers play a crucial role in facilitating the buying and selling of precious metals in the global market. They provide the necessary infrastructure, tools, and services for traders and investors to access the market and execute their trades. Here's an overview of trading platforms and brokers for precious metals trading:

Trading platforms: A trading platform is a software application that enables market participants to place orders, manage their positions, and access market data, news, and analysis. Various trading platforms cater to different types of traders and investors, offering a range of features, such as advanced charting tools, technical indicators, and customizable user interfaces. Some popular trading platforms for precious metals include MetaTrader 4 (MT4), MetaTrader 5 (MT5), and TradingView. When selecting a trading platform, it's essential to consider factors such as ease of use, available features, compatibility with your broker, and any associated costs.

Brokers: Brokers act as intermediaries between market participants and the various markets for precious metals trading, such as the spot market, futures market, and options market. Brokers can be categorised into two main types: full-service brokers and discount brokers. Full-service brokers provide a comprehensive range of services, including trade execution, research, market analysis, and personalised advice, while discount brokers primarily focus on trade execution at a lower cost.

When selecting a broker for precious metals trading, consider the following factors:

- Regulatory compliance: Choose a broker that is regulated by a reputable financial authority, such as the U.S. Commodity Futures Trading Commission (CFTC), the UK's Financial Conduct Authority (FCA), or the Australian Securities and Investments Commission (ASIC). This ensures that the broker adheres to strict regulatory standards and provides a secure trading environment.

- Trading fees and costs: Compare the fees and costs associated with trading precious metals, such as spreads, commissions, and any additional charges for using trading platforms or accessing market data. Lower trading costs can significantly impact your overall profitability.

- Execution quality and speed: Assess the quality and speed of trade execution provided by the broker. Fast and reliable trade execution is crucial for taking advantage of short-term market opportunities.

- Range of available instruments: Ensure that the broker offers a variety of trading instruments for precious metals, such as spot contracts, futures contracts, options, and ETFs. This provides you with greater flexibility in your trading strategies.

- Customer service and support: Evaluate the quality of customer service and support provided by the broker. Reliable and responsive customer support can be invaluable in addressing any technical issues or concerns that may arise during your trading activities.

Order Types and Execution

Understanding order types and their execution is essential for effectively managing risk and implementing trading strategies in the precious metals market. Various order types allow traders to control when and how their trades are executed, providing flexibility and precision in their trading decisions.

Here's an overview of the common order types and their execution:

Market order: A market order is an instruction to buy or sell a precious metal at the best available price in the market. Market orders are executed immediately and are typically used when a trader wants to enter or exit a position quickly. While market orders guarantee execution, they do not guarantee a specific price, which may lead to slippage, particularly in fast-moving or illiquid markets.

Limit order: A limit order is an instruction to buy or sell a precious metal at a specified price or better. Limit orders allow traders to define the maximum price they are willing to pay when buying or the minimum price they are willing to accept when selling. Limit orders provide control over the execution price but do not guarantee execution, as the market may not reach the specified price.

Stop order: A stop order, also known as a stop-loss order, is an instruction to buy or sell a precious metal when the market price reaches a specified level. Stop orders are typically used to protect against significant losses or to lock in profits on an existing position. When the stop price is reached, the stop order becomes a market order and is executed at the best available price. This type of order helps manage risk but does not guarantee a specific execution price, which may result in slippage.

Stop-limit order: A stop-limit order combines the features of a stop order and a limit order. is an instruction to buy or sell a precious metal when the market price reaches a specified stop level, but only if the order can be executed within a specified price range (the limit). Stop-limit orders provide control over the execution price and help manage risk, but they do not guarantee execution, as the market may not trade within the specified price range.

Trailing stop order: A trailing stop order is a type of stop order that moves with the market price, maintaining a specified distance (either in points or percentage) from the current market price. As the market price moves in a favourable direction, the trailing stop adjusts accordingly, helping to lock in profits and protect against losses. If the market price moves against the position, the trailing stop remains fixed, and the order is executed when the stop price is reached. Trailing stop orders do not guarantee a specific execution price and may result in slippage.

One-Cancels-the-Other (OCO) order: An OCO order consists of two orders, a limit order and a stop order, placed simultaneously. If one of the orders is executed, the other order is automatically cancelled. This type of order is useful for traders who want to take advantage of different market scenarios while managing their risk exposure.

Leverage and Margin

Leverage and margin are essential concepts for traders and investors participating in the precious metals market, as they allow for greater exposure to price movements with a smaller initial investment. Understanding how leverage and margin work is crucial for managing risk and maximising the potential returns on your trades. Here's an overview of leverage and margin in precious metals trading:

Leverage

Leverage is the use of borrowed funds to increase your exposure to a particular market or asset, such as precious metals. In trading, leverage is often expressed as a ratio, such as 50:1 or 100:1, indicating the amount of borrowed funds you can control for each unit of your own capital. Leverage allows traders to amplify their gains on successful trades, but it also magnifies losses on unsuccessful trades. It is essential to use leverage responsibly and be aware of the potential risks associated with it.

Margin

Margin is the initial amount of capital required to open a leveraged position in the market. It serves as collateral for the borrowed funds used in a leveraged trade. The margin requirement is typically expressed as a percentage of the total trade value, such as 2% or 5%. Margin requirements vary depending on the asset being traded, the level of leverage used, and the broker's policies.

There are two main types of margin in trading:

Initial margin

The initial margin is the minimum amount of capital required to open a new leveraged position. It is calculated as a percentage of the total trade value and must be maintained in your trading account for the duration of the trade.

Maintenance margin

The maintenance margin is the minimum amount of capital that must be maintained in your trading account to keep a leveraged position open. If your account balance falls below the maintenance margin level, you may receive a margin call from your broker, requiring you to deposit additional funds or close some or all of your positions to meet the margin requirements.

Margin trading can be a powerful tool for traders and investors looking to maximise their potential returns in the precious metals market. However, trading on margin also carries inherent risks, as it amplifies both profits and losses. It is crucial to understand the margin requirements set by your broker, monitor your account balance and margin levels closely, and employ sound risk management strategies to protect your capital.

Bid and Ask Prices

Bid and ask prices are fundamental concepts in the precious metals market, as they represent the prices at which market participants are willing to buy and sell these assets. Understanding bid and ask prices is essential for executing trades, calculating spreads, and evaluating the liquidity of the market. Here's an overview of bid and ask prices in precious metals trading:

Bid price

The bid price is the highest price that a buyer is willing to pay for a specific quantity of a precious metal. It represents the demand side of the market and is the price at which you, as a seller, can sell your asset. The bid price is typically lower than the ask price, as buyers want to purchase the asset at the lowest possible price.

Ask price

The ask price, also known as the offer price, is the lowest price at which a seller is willing to sell a specific quantity of a precious metal. It represents the supply side of the market and is the price at which you, as a buyer, can purchase the asset. The ask price is typically higher than the bid price, as sellers want to sell the asset at the highest possible price.

Bid-ask spread

The difference between the bid price and the ask price is known as the bid-ask spread. The spread represents the cost of trading in the market and is influenced by factors such as liquidity, volatility, and market conditions. In general, a narrower bid-ask spread indicates a more liquid market, as it reflects a higher level of trading activity and competition among market participants.

Price quotes

Precious metals prices are typically quoted in two parts: the bid price and the ask price. For example, a quote for gold might be expressed as "1,850.00/1,850.50," where the bid price is $1,850.00, and the ask price is $1,850.50. The bid-ask spread in this example would be $0.50.

Understanding bid and ask prices is essential for effectively navigating the precious metals market and executing your trades. By monitoring bid and ask prices, you can gain insights into the market's liquidity, volatility, and potential trading opportunities. It is also important to consider the impact of bid-ask spreads on your trading costs and overall profitability, as tighter spreads can reduce your transaction costs and improve your chances of success.

Factors Influencing Precious Metals Prices

Supply and demand dynamics play a crucial role in determining the prices of precious metals in the global market. Understanding these dynamics can provide traders and investors with valuable insights into the factors that drive price movements and help them make more informed trading decisions. Here's an overview of the key supply and demand factors that influence precious metals prices:

Production and mining: The supply of precious metals is primarily determined by the production and mining activities of various countries and companies. Factors such as mining costs, environmental regulations, technological advancements, and geopolitical events can impact the production levels of precious metals. For example, disruptions in mining operations due to labour strikes, natural disasters, or political instability can lead to reduced supply and higher prices.

Recycling and scrap: The recycling of precious metals from scrap materials, such as electronic waste and used jewellery, is another source of supply in the market. The availability and cost of recycling can influence the overall supply of precious metals and their prices. In times of high prices, the recycling of scrap materials can increase, providing an additional source of supply to the market.

Industrial demand: Precious metals such as silver, platinum, and palladium have a wide range of industrial applications, including electronics, automotive manufacturing, and chemical processes. Changes in the global economy and technological advancements can impact the industrial demand for these metals, influencing their prices. For example, increased adoption of electric vehicles can lead to higher demand for platinum and palladium, which are used in catalytic converters.

Investment demand: Investment demand for precious metals, particularly gold and silver, is driven by factors such as market sentiment, inflation expectations, and geopolitical events. Investors often turn to precious metals as a store of value and a hedge against economic uncertainty, currency devaluation, and inflation. During periods of financial market volatility or economic instability, the demand for precious metals may increase, driving up their prices. Central bank activity: Central banks play a significant role in the precious metals market, as they hold large reserves of gold and can influence its price through their buying and selling activities. Central banks may adjust their gold reserves as a part of their monetary policy or in response to changes in the global economic environment. Their actions can have a substantial impact on the demand for gold and, consequently, its price.

Exchange rates: Precious metals are typically priced in US dollars, so fluctuations in exchange rates can influence their prices. A weaker US dollar can make precious metals more affordable for investors holding other currencies, increasing demand and driving up prices. Conversely, a stronger US dollar can make precious metals more expensive for investors in other currencies, potentially reducing demand and leading to lower prices.

Economic Indicators and their Impact on Precious Metals

Economic indicators provide valuable insights into the health of the global economy and can have a significant impact on precious metals prices. Understanding the relationship between economic indicators and precious metals prices can help traders and investors make more informed decisions and identify potential market opportunities. Here's an overview of key economic indicators and their impact on precious metals:

Inflation: Inflation represents the rate at which the general price level of goods and services is rising over time. Precious metals, particularly gold, are often considered a hedge against inflation, as they tend to maintain their value or appreciate during periods of high inflation. As a result, when inflation expectations rise, the demand for precious metals may increase, driving up their prices.

Interest rates: Interest rates, set by central banks, influence the cost of borrowing and the returns on various investment assets. When interest rates are low, the opportunity cost of holding non-interest-bearing assets, such as gold, decreases, potentially increasing demand for precious metals. Conversely, when interest rates rise, higher-yielding assets may become more attractive to investors, leading to reduced demand for precious metals and lower prices.

Gross Domestic Product (GDP): GDP is a measure of the economic output of a country and is an indicator of its overall economic health. Strong GDP growth can lead to increased industrial demand for precious metals, such as silver, platinum, and palladium, driving up their prices. On the other hand, weak GDP growth or economic contraction may result in reduced industrial demand for these metals and lower prices.

Unemployment rate: The unemployment rate measures the percentage of the labour force that is without work. High unemployment can lead to reduced consumer spending and lower economic growth, potentially impacting the demand for precious metals and their prices. Conversely, low unemployment can signal a healthy economy and increased consumer spending, which may boost industrial demand for precious metals and support higher prices.

Consumer Confidence Index (CCI): The CCI is a measure of consumer sentiment and their expectations about future economic conditions. High consumer confidence can indicate a strong economy and increased spending, potentially leading to higher demand for precious metals and their prices. On the other hand, low consumer confidence may signal economic uncertainty and reduced spending, which can negatively impact precious metals prices.

By monitoring economic indicators and understanding their potential impact on precious metals prices, traders and investors can better anticipate market trends and make more informed decisions when buying or selling these assets. It is important to stay updated on global economic developments and incorporate this information into your trading strategies and investment decisions.

Geopolitical Events

Geopolitical events play a crucial role in shaping the global economy and financial markets, and they can have a significant impact on precious metals prices. In times of uncertainty or heightened geopolitical risk, investors often turn to precious metals as a safe haven, increasing demand and driving up prices. Here's an overview of the influence of geopolitical events on precious metals:

Wars and conflicts: Wars and armed conflicts can create uncertainty in financial markets and disrupt global trade, potentially affecting the supply and demand dynamics of precious metals. For example, during the Ukraine-Russia war, concerns about potential disruptions to the supply of metals, such as palladium and platinum, from Russia (a significant producer of these metals) led to increased demand and higher prices for these assets. Additionally, the overall uncertainty surrounding the conflict led to a flight to safety, with investors seeking refuge in gold as a safe-haven asset.

Political instability: Political instability, such as government upheavals, protests, or elections, can create uncertainty in the markets and impact the global economy. These events can lead to changes in trade policies, currency values, and investor sentiment, which can, in turn, influence the demand for precious metals and their prices.

Trade disputes and sanctions: Trade disputes, such as tariffs or trade wars, can disrupt the flow of goods and services between countries, affecting the global economy and the demand for precious metals. Sanctions imposed by one country on another can also impact the supply of precious metals, as they may limit the ability of affected countries to produce or export these assets. For instance, sanctions imposed on Russia due to its actions in Ukraine could potentially affect the supply of precious metals in the global market, influencing their prices.

Currency crises: Currency crises, such as sharp devaluations or the collapse of a currency, can lead to economic turmoil and increased demand for precious metals as a store of value. Investors may turn to gold and other precious metals as a hedge against currency risk during these times, driving up prices.

International relations and treaties: International relations and treaties can also influence the precious metals market by affecting trade policies, currency values, and global economic growth. Changes in these relationships or the implementation of new treaties can create both opportunities and challenges for precious metals investors, as they can impact supply, demand, and prices.

By closely monitoring geopolitical events and understanding their potential impact on precious metals prices, traders and investors can better anticipate market trends and make more informed decisions when buying or selling these assets. It is crucial to stay updated on global events and incorporate this information into your trading strategies and investment decisions to navigate the markets effectively during times of heightened geopolitical risk.

Central Bank Policies

Central bank policies play a critical role in shaping the global economy and financial markets, and they can have a significant impact on precious metals prices. Understanding the influence of central bank policies on precious metals can help traders and investors make more informed decisions and identify potential market opportunities.

Here's an overview of key central bank policies and their impact on precious metals:

Interest rates: Central banks set interest rates to influence the cost of borrowing and the returns on various investment assets. Changes in interest rates can affect the demand for precious metals, particularly gold, as they influence the opportunity cost of holding non-interest-bearing assets. When interest rates are low, the opportunity cost of holding gold decreases, potentially increasing its demand and driving up prices. Conversely, when interest rates rise, higher-yielding assets may become more attractive to investors, leading to reduced demand for precious metals and lower prices.

Quantitative easing (QE): Quantitative easing is a monetary policy tool used by central banks to stimulate economic growth by purchasing government bonds and other financial assets. This policy increases the money supply, lowers long-term interest rates, and encourages borrowing and investment. However, QE can also lead to concerns about inflation and currency devaluation, which can boost demand for precious metals as a hedge against these risks, driving up prices.

Gold reserves: Central banks hold significant gold reserves as a part of their foreign exchange reserves, and their buying and selling activities can have a substantial impact on gold prices. Central banks may adjust their gold reserves to diversify their holdings, manage exchange rate risk, or respond to changes in the global economic environment. Large-scale purchases or sales of gold by central banks can influence market sentiment and affect gold prices.

Currency interventions: Central banks may intervene in foreign exchange markets to influence the value of their currency, either by buying or selling their currency or by adjusting interest rates. As precious metals are typically priced in US dollars, fluctuations in exchange rates can influence their prices. A weaker US dollar can make precious metals more affordable for investors holding other currencies, increasing demand and driving up prices. Conversely, a stronger US dollar can make precious metals more expensive for investors in other currencies, potentially reducing demand and leading to lower prices.

Forward guidance: Central banks often provide forward guidance on their future monetary policy actions, which can influence market expectations and investor sentiment. Forward guidance on interest rates, inflation expectations, or other policy measures can impact the demand for precious metals, as investors adjust their portfolios in anticipation of changes in the economic environment.

Currency Fluctuations

Currency fluctuations, also known as exchange rate movements, can have a significant impact on precious metals prices, as these assets are typically priced in US dollars. Understanding the relationship between currency fluctuations and precious metals prices can help traders and investors make more informed decisions and identify potential market opportunities.

Here's an overview of how currency fluctuations influence precious metals prices:

US dollar strength: A stronger US dollar can make precious metals more expensive for investors holding other currencies, as they need to spend more of their local currency to buy the same amount of the metal. This increased cost can reduce demand for precious metals, leading to lower prices. Conversely, a weaker US dollar can make precious metals more affordable for investors in other currencies, potentially increasing demand and driving up prices.

Carry trade and interest rates: Currency fluctuations can be influenced by interest rate differentials between countries, which can impact the demand for precious metals. For example, when interest rates are higher in one country compared to another, investors may engage in carry trade strategies by borrowing in the lower-yielding currency and investing in the higher-yielding currency. These strategies can lead to appreciation or depreciation of the involved currencies, which can, in turn, impact precious metals prices.

Economic indicators and market sentiment: Currency fluctuations are often influenced by economic indicators, such as GDP growth, inflation, and employment data, as well as market sentiment and risk appetite. Strong economic data and positive market sentiment can lead to appreciation of a currency, which can affect precious metals prices. On the other hand, weak economic data and negative market sentiment can lead to depreciation of a currency, potentially influencing precious metals prices.

Central bank interventions: Central banks may intervene in foreign exchange markets to influence the value of their currency, either by buying or selling their currency or by adjusting interest rates. These interventions can lead to fluctuations in exchange rates, which can influence the prices of precious metals. For example, a central bank's efforts to devalue its currency can make precious metals more expensive in that currency, potentially reducing demand and lowering prices.

Geopolitical events: Geopolitical events, such as wars, political instability, and trade disputes, can create uncertainty in financial markets and affect currency values. These events can lead to fluctuations in exchange rates, which can, in turn, influence precious metals prices. For instance, during times of heightened geopolitical risk, investors may seek refuge in safe-haven currencies, such as the US dollar, leading to appreciation of the currency and potential impacts on precious metals prices.

Investment Demand

Investment demand is a significant factor influencing precious metals prices, as investors buy these assets for various reasons, such as portfolio diversification, wealth preservation, or as a hedge against inflation and economic uncertainty. Understanding the factors driving investment demand for precious metals can help traders and investors make more informed decisions and identify potential market opportunities.

Here's an overview of the key drivers of investment demand for precious metals:

Portfolio diversification: Many investors include precious metals in their portfolios as a means of diversification, as these assets often exhibit low or negative correlation with traditional investments, such as stocks and bonds. By allocating a portion of their portfolio to precious metals, investors can potentially reduce overall portfolio risk and enhance long-term returns.

Wealth preservation: Precious metals, particularly gold, are considered a store of value and a means of wealth preservation. Investors may turn to gold and other precious metals during times of economic uncertainty or market volatility to protect their wealth from potential losses in other asset classes.

Inflation hedge: Precious metals are often seen as a hedge against inflation, as their prices tend to maintain their value or appreciate during periods of high inflation. When inflation expectations rise, investors may increase their allocation to precious metals to protect their purchasing power, driving up demand and prices.

Safe-haven demand: In times of geopolitical tension, economic uncertainty, or financial market turmoil, investors often seek refuge in safe-haven assets, such as gold, to protect their wealth from potential losses. This increased demand for safe-haven assets can drive up the prices of precious metals.

Speculation: Some investors trade precious metals for speculative purposes, seeking to profit from short-term price fluctuations. Speculative demand can contribute to price volatility in the precious metals market, as traders buy or sell these assets in response to market signals, economic data, or technical analysis.

Exchange-traded funds (ETFs) and other investment products: The growth of ETFs and other investment products that track precious metals prices has made it easier for investors to gain exposure to these assets. Increased demand for these investment products can result in increased demand for the underlying precious metals, influencing their prices.

By understanding the factors driving investment demand for precious metals, traders and investors can better anticipate market trends and make more informed decisions when buying or selling these assets. It is essential to monitor global economic developments, investor sentiment, and market trends to stay ahead of potential shifts in investment demand for precious metals.

Technical Analysis for Precious Metals Trading

Chart types and timeframes

Technical analysis is an essential tool for precious metals traders, as it helps them identify trends, support and resistance levels, and potential entry and exit points for their trades. Chart types and timeframes play a crucial role in technical analysis, as they provide different perspectives on price movements and market activity. Here's an overview of common chart types and timeframes used in technical analysis for precious metals trading:

Chart types:

A. **Line Chart:** A line chart is the simplest type of chart, representing the closing price of a precious metal over a specified period. By connecting the closing prices with a continuous line, this chart offers a clear view of the overall price trend.

B. **Bar Chart:** A bar chart provides more detailed information about the price movement of a precious metal during a specific time interval. Each bar represents the open, high, low, and close (OHLC) prices for the period, allowing traders to visualise the price range and volatility.

C. **Candlestick Chart:** Similar to bar charts, candlestick charts display the OHLC prices for a given period but represent the data in a more visually appealing format. Candlesticks show the relationship between the opening and closing prices through the use of coloured bodies, making it easier to identify bullish or bearish price movements.

D. **Point and Figure Chart:** Point and Figure charts focus on price changes and ignore the time aspect, making them unique compared to other chart types. This chart type plots price movements in columns of X's (rising prices) and O's (falling prices) and is primarily used for identifying support and resistance levels and chart patterns.

Timeframes

Intraday

Intraday timeframes, such as 1-minute, 5-minute, or 1-hour charts, focus on short-term price movements and are commonly used by day traders and scalpers who aim to capitalise on quick market fluctuations.

Daily

Daily charts represent the OHLC prices for each trading day, providing a more comprehensive view of the market compared to intraday timeframes. These charts are popular among swing traders and short-term investors who base their trading decisions on daily price trends.

Weekly

Weekly charts display the OHLC prices for each week, offering a broader perspective on price trends and market activity. This timeframe is often used by medium- to long-term investors and traders who focus on the larger market trends and potential turning points.

Monthly

Monthly charts represent the OHLC prices for each month, providing a long-term view of the market and highlighting significant historical price levels and trends. This timeframe is suitable for long-term investors and traders who aim to identify major market trends and make strategic investment decisions.

By selecting the appropriate chart type and timeframe, traders can tailor their technical analysis to suit their trading style and objectives. It is essential to choose the right combination of chart types and timeframes to analyse price movements effectively and make informed trading decisions in the precious metals market.

Trend Identification and Analysis

Identifying and analysing trends is a fundamental aspect of technical analysis, as it helps traders determine the overall market direction and make informed decisions regarding their trades. Recognizing trends in precious metals prices can provide valuable insights into potential entry and exit points for trades. Here's an overview of trend identification and analysis techniques commonly used in precious metals trading:

Uptrend: An uptrend is characterised by a series of higher highs and higher lows, indicating that the overall market direction is upward. In an uptrend, buying opportunities may arise as the price pulls back to a support level, such as a trendline or moving average, before resuming its upward movement.

Downtrend: A downtrend is characterised by a series of lower highs and lower lows, signifying that the overall market direction is downward. In a downtrend, selling opportunities may present themselves as the price bounces back to a resistance level, such as a trendline or moving average, before continuing its downward trajectory.

Sideways trend (consolidation): A sideways trend, or consolidation, occurs when the market is trading within a relatively narrow range, with neither buyers nor sellers gaining control. During a consolidation phase, traders may look for potential breakouts or reversals to capitalise on new trends.

Trendlines: Trendlines are diagonal lines drawn on a price chart to connect successive highs or lows, helping traders visualise the direction of the trend. An upward trendline connects higher lows, acting as a support level, while a downward trendline connects lower highs, serving as a resistance level. Trendlines can be used to identify potential entry and exit points and to gauge the strength of a trend.

Moving averages: Moving averages smooth out price data over a specific period, helping traders identify trends and potential support or resistance levels. Commonly used moving averages include the simple moving average (SMA) and the exponential moving average (EMA). Traders may use single or multiple moving averages to identify trends, with shorter-term moving averages providing a more sensitive indication of the current trend and longer-term moving averages offering a smoother perspective of the overall trend direction.

Trend indicators: There are several trend indicators that traders can use to identify and analyse trends in the precious metals market. Some popular trend indicators include the Moving Average Convergence Divergence (MACD), the Average Directional Index (ADX), and the Parabolic SAR. These indicators can help traders confirm the direction and strength of a trend, as well as identify potential trend reversals or continuations.

By identifying and analysing trends in the precious metals market, traders can better anticipate price movements and make more informed decisions when entering or exiting trades. Incorporating trend analysis techniques into your trading strategy can help you determine the most favourable market conditions for your trades and enhance your overall trading performance.

Support and Resistance Levels

Support and resistance levels are critical concepts in technical analysis, as they help traders identify potential price reversal or continuation points in the market. Understanding support and resistance levels can provide valuable insights into the supply and demand dynamics of precious metals and assist traders in making more informed decisions regarding their trades. Here's an overview of support and resistance levels and how they can be used in precious metals trading:

Support levels: A support level is a price at which buying pressure tends to be strong enough to prevent the price from falling further. Support levels can be identified by analysing historical price data and noting areas where the price has previously stalled or reversed its downward movement. Support levels act as a floor for the market, offering potential buying opportunities as traders anticipate a price bounce or reversal at these levels.

Resistance levels: A resistance level is a price at which selling pressure tends to be strong enough to prevent the price from rising further. Resistance levels can be identified by analysing historical price data and noting areas where the price has previously stalled or reversed its upward movement. Resistance levels act as a ceiling for the market, offering potential selling opportunities as traders anticipate a price retracement or reversal at these levels.

Horizontal support and resistance: Horizontal support and resistance levels are identified by drawing horizontal lines on a price chart at levels where the price has repeatedly failed to move higher or lower. These levels indicate areas of strong buying or selling interest, as market participants have previously shown a willingness to enter or exit positions at these prices.

Trendline support and resistance: Trendlines can also act as support and resistance levels, as they connect successive highs or lows and indicate potential price barriers. An upward trendline connecting higher lows serves as a support level, while a downward trendline connecting lower highs acts as a resistance level. Traders may use these trendlines to identify potential entry and exit points for their trades.

Moving average support and resistance: Moving averages, such as the simple moving average (SMA) or exponential moving average (EMA), can also act as dynamic support or resistance levels. When the price is above a moving average, the moving average may act as a support level, and when the price is below a moving average, the moving average may serve as a resistance level.

Psychological support and resistance: Round numbers, such as $1,000, $1,500, or $2,000, can also act as psychological support and resistance levels, as market participants tend to place greater importance on these levels when making trading decisions.

Technical Indicators

Technical indicators are mathematical calculations based on price, volume, or open interest data that help traders identify trends, support and resistance levels, overbought or oversold conditions, and potential entry and exit points in the market. There are numerous technical indicators available, each with its unique methodology and purpose. Here's an overview of some popular technical indicators used in precious metals trading:

Moving Averages (MA): Moving averages, such as the simple moving average (SMA) and exponential moving average (EMA), smooth out price data over a specified period to help traders identify trends and potential support or resistance levels. Traders may use single or multiple moving averages to generate buy or sell signals when the price crosses above or below the moving average line.

Relative Strength Index (RSI): The RSI is a momentum oscillator that measures the speed and change of price movements on a scale of 0 to 100. The RSI is typically used to identify overbought or oversold conditions in the market, with readings above 70 indicating overbought conditions and readings below 30 signalling oversold conditions. Traders may use the RSI to generate buy or sell signals based on these levels or to confirm the strength of a trend.

Moving Average Convergence Divergence (MACD): The MACD is a trend-following momentum indicator that shows the relationship between two moving averages of a security's price. The MACD is calculated by subtracting the longer-term moving average (usually 26-day EMA) from the shorter-term moving average (usually 12-day EMA). Traders may use the MACD to generate buy or sell signals when the MACD line crosses above or below the signal line, which is typically a 9-day EMA of the MACD.

Bollinger Bands: Bollinger Bands are a volatility indicator that consists of a simple moving average (usually a 20-day SMA) and two standard deviation bands above and below the moving average. The bands expand and contract based on market volatility, with wider bands indicating higher volatility and narrower bands indicating lower volatility. Traders may use Bollinger Bands to identify overbought or oversold conditions, potential trend reversals, or price breakouts.

Stochastic Oscillator: The Stochastic Oscillator is a momentum indicator that compares a security's closing price to its price range over a specified period. The Stochastic Oscillator consists of two lines – the %K line and the %D line – and ranges from 0 to 100. Traders may use the Stochastic Oscillator to identify overbought or oversold conditions, with readings above 80 indicating overbought conditions and readings below 20 signalling oversold conditions. Buy or sell signals may be generated when the %K line crosses above or below the %D line.

By incorporating technical indicators into your trading strategy, you can enhance your market analysis and make more informed decisions when trading precious metals. It is essential to understand the strengths and limitations of each indicator and to combine them with other technical and fundamental analysis techniques for a comprehensive trading approach.

Chart Patterns and Formations

Chart patterns and formations are essential tools in technical analysis, as they help traders identify potential trend reversals or continuations and provide valuable insights into market psychology. Recognizing chart patterns and formations can assist traders in anticipating future price movements and making more informed decisions when entering or exiting trades in the precious metals market.

Here's an overview of some common chart patterns and formations used in precious metals trading:

Reversal Patterns: Reversal patterns signal a potential change in the prevailing trend and can be either bullish or bearish, depending on the prior trend.

- **Head and Shoulders:** A head and shoulders pattern is a bearish reversal pattern characterised by three peaks – a higher peak (head) between two lower peaks (shoulders). This pattern is completed when the price breaks below the neckline, which is a support level connecting the lows between the head and the shoulders.

- **Inverse Head and Shoulders:** An inverse head and shoulders pattern is a bullish reversal pattern that is the opposite of the head and shoulders pattern. It is characterised by three troughs – a lower trough (head) between two higher troughs (shoulders). The pattern is completed when the price breaks above the neckline, a resistance level connecting the highs between the head and the shoulders.

Continuation Patterns: Continuation patterns indicate a temporary pause in the prevailing trend, suggesting that the trend will resume once the pattern is completed.

- **Flags:** Flags are short-term continuation patterns that resemble a small rectangle sloping against the prevailing trend. A flag indicates a brief consolidation period before the trend continues in its original direction.

- **Pennants:** Pennants are similar to flags but have a small symmetrical triangle shape instead of a rectangular shape. Like flags, pennants suggest a brief consolidation before the trend resumes.

- **Triangles:** Triangles are continuation patterns that can be ascending, descending, or symmetrical. They are characterised by converging trendlines that enclose the price action, indicating a period of consolidation before the price breaks out in the direction of the prevailing trend.

Breakout Patterns: Breakout patterns occur when the price moves beyond a significant support or resistance level, indicating a potential acceleration in the prevailing trend.

- Cup and Handle: A cup and handle pattern is a bullish continuation pattern that resembles a tea cup with a handle. The cup represents a rounded bottom, followed by a small consolidation (handle) that slopes downward. The pattern is completed when the price breaks above the resistance level at the top of the handle, signalling a continuation of the uptrend.

- Double Top/Double Bottom: Double top and double bottom patterns are reversal patterns that occur when the price encounters a significant resistance (double top) or support (double bottom) level twice and fails to break through. A double top pattern signals a bearish trend reversal, while a double bottom pattern suggests a bullish trend reversal.

By identifying and analysing chart patterns and formations, traders can better anticipate potential price movements and make more informed decisions when entering or exiting trades in the precious metals market. Combining chart pattern analysis with other technical and fundamental analysis techniques can help traders develop a comprehensive trading strategy and improve their overall trading performance.

Macro and Micro Economic Factors

Fundamental analysis is a critical component of precious metals trading, as it helps traders understand the underlying forces that drive the market. Both macro and microeconomic factors can significantly influence the prices of precious metals, and understanding these factors can provide valuable insights into the supply and demand dynamics of the market. Here's an overview of some key macro and microeconomic factors to consider when trading precious metals:

Macro Factors

- **Economic Growth:** Gross Domestic Product (GDP) growth can influence precious metals prices, as it reflects the overall health of an economy. Strong economic growth may lead to increased industrial demand for metals like silver, platinum, and palladium, pushing prices higher. Conversely, weak economic growth may result in lower demand, putting downward pressure on prices.

- **Interest Rates:** Central bank interest rate policies can impact precious metals prices as higher interest rates generally increase the opportunity cost of holding non-interest-bearing assets like gold and silver. Conversely, low interest rates can make precious metals more attractive to investors, as the opportunity cost of holding them decreases.

- **Inflation:** Precious metals are often considered a hedge against inflation. When inflation is high or expected to rise, investors may turn to precious metals to preserve their wealth, driving prices higher. On the other hand, low or stable inflation may reduce the demand for precious metals, leading to lower prices.

- **Currency Fluctuations:** Precious metals are typically priced in US dollars, making their prices sensitive to fluctuations in the value of the dollar. A strong dollar can put downward pressure on precious metals prices, as it makes them more expensive for buyers using other currencies. Conversely, a weak dollar can support higher precious metals prices.

Micro Factors

- **Supply and Demand:** The balance between supply and demand is a crucial factor in determining precious metals prices. Factors influencing supply include mining output, recycling, and central bank sales, while factors affecting demand include industrial usage, jewellery fabrication, and investment demand. Imbalances between supply and demand can lead to significant price fluctuations.

- **Production Costs:** The cost of producing precious metals can impact their prices. High production costs may result in reduced mining output, limiting supply and potentially driving prices higher. Conversely, low production costs can lead to increased supply, putting downward pressure on prices.

- **Technological Advancements:** Technological innovations can affect the demand for precious metals, as they may lead to new applications or increased efficiency in existing uses. For example, advances in battery technology can increase the demand for metals like platinum and palladium, which are used in catalytic converters and fuel cells.

- **Market Sentiment:** Investor sentiment and market psychology can play a significant role in driving precious metals prices. Factors such as risk appetite, market uncertainty, and geopolitical events can influence investor sentiment, leading to fluctuations in demand for precious metals as safe-haven or speculative assets.

By considering both macro and microeconomic factors in your fundamental analysis, you can gain a more comprehensive understanding of the forces driving the precious metals market and make more informed trading decisions. Combining fundamental analysis with technical analysis can further enhance your trading strategy and improve your overall performance in the precious metals market.

Industry Trends and Developments

Keeping up with industry trends and developments is crucial for precious metals traders, as these factors can have a significant impact on supply, demand, and prices. Understanding emerging trends and staying informed about recent developments can help traders anticipate potential shifts in the market and make more informed decisions when trading precious metals. Here's an overview of some key industry trends and developments to consider when trading precious metals:

Mining Operations and Exploration: Changes in mining output, new discoveries, and shifts in production costs can all influence the supply of precious metals. Monitoring mining operations, exploration activities, and technological advancements in mining techniques can provide valuable insights into potential shifts in precious metals supply.
Recycling: Recycling is an essential source of supply for precious metals, particularly for platinum and palladium used in automotive catalysts. Trends in recycling rates and developments in recycling technologies can impact the overall supply of precious metals, influencing prices.

Technological Innovations: Technological advancements can create new applications for precious metals or improve their efficiency in existing applications, leading to shifts in demand. For example, developments in renewable energy, electronics, and medical applications can have a significant impact on the demand for precious metals.

Environmental and Regulatory Changes: Changes in environmental regulations and policies can affect the precious metals industry, influencing production costs, mining operations, and recycling efforts. Monitoring changes in environmental policies and regulations can help traders anticipate potential shifts in supply and demand.

Geopolitical Events: Geopolitical events, such as wars, political tensions, and trade disputes, can impact the global economy and influence investor sentiment, leading to fluctuations in demand for precious metals as safe-haven or speculative assets. Keeping up with geopolitical developments can help traders better understand the potential impact on precious metals prices.

Central Bank Policies: Central banks play a significant role in the precious metals market, as their policies can impact interest rates, inflation, and currency values, all of which can influence precious metals prices. Monitoring central bank policies and actions can help traders anticipate potential shifts in the market.

Market Sentiment: Staying informed about investor sentiment and market psychology is crucial for precious metals traders, as these factors can drive demand for precious metals as safe-haven or speculative assets. Monitoring financial news, economic indicators, and investor behaviour can help traders better understand market sentiment and its potential impact on precious metals prices.

Analysing Financial Statements and Reports

While analysing financial statements and reports is more commonly associated with stock trading, it can also be helpful when trading precious metals, particularly when trading stocks of mining companies or ETFs focused on precious metals. Understanding a company's financial health and performance can provide valuable insights into the overall health of the precious metals industry and potential shifts in supply and demand dynamics.

Here's an overview of some key aspects to consider when analysing financial statements and reports for precious metals trading:

Income Statement: The income statement provides information on a company's revenues, expenses, and profits over a specific period. Key metrics to examine include revenue growth, gross margin, operating margin, and net income. By comparing these metrics across different companies and time periods, traders can gain insights into industry trends and the overall health of the precious metals sector.

Balance Sheet: The balance sheet provides a snapshot of a company's financial position at a specific point in time, detailing its assets, liabilities, and shareholders' equity. Important metrics to consider include current assets, current liabilities, total assets, total liabilities, and the debt-to-equity ratio. A strong balance sheet can indicate a financially healthy company, while a weak balance sheet may signal potential financial troubles.

Cash Flow Statement: The cash flow statement shows a company's cash inflows and outflows over a specific period, providing insights into its liquidity and financial health. Key metrics to examine include operating cash flow, investing cash flow, and financing cash flow. Positive cash flow from operations can indicate a healthy and sustainable business, while negative cash flow may signal potential financial difficulties.

Management Discussion and Analysis (MD&A): The MD&A section of a company's annual report provides management's perspective on the company's financial performance, business trends, and future outlook. Analysing the MD&A can help traders gain a deeper understanding of a company's operations, competitive landscape, and growth prospects within the precious metals industry.

Earnings Calls and Presentations: Earnings calls and presentations offer an opportunity for company management to discuss financial results, business developments, and future plans with investors and analysts. Listening to earnings calls and reviewing presentation materials can provide valuable insights into a company's performance, industry trends, and potential risks and opportunities within the precious metals sector.

By analysing financial statements and reports, traders can gain a deeper understanding of the health of the precious metals industry and the performance of individual companies within the sector. Combining this information with technical and fundamental analysis can help traders make more informed decisions when trading precious metals, mining stocks, or related ETFs.

Building a Successful Precious Metals Trading Career
Developing your unique trading style

Building a successful career in precious metals trading requires not only knowledge and skills but also the development of a unique trading style that suits your personality, risk tolerance, and financial goals.

Here are some steps to help you develop your unique trading style:

Self-assessment: Begin by evaluating your personality traits, strengths, and weaknesses. Are you more analytical or intuitive? Do you prefer taking risks or playing it safe? Understanding your natural inclinations can help you tailor your trading style to your personality and preferences.

Define your goals: Clearly outline your financial goals and time horizon. Are you looking to generate income, grow your capital, or hedge against risks? Knowing your objectives will help you choose the appropriate trading strategies and instruments.

Choose your preferred markets: Decide which precious metals you want to focus on – gold, silver, platinum, or palladium. Each metal has its unique characteristics, and some traders may find it more comfortable to focus on one or two specific markets rather than trying to trade all of them.

Learn from others: Study successful traders and their trading styles. Understand what makes them successful and consider whether their approach might be suitable for you. Don try to copy them, but use their strategies as inspiration to develop your own.

Experiment with strategies: Try out various trading strategies and techniques, such as trend-following, mean reversion, or breakout trading. Evaluate the performance of each strategy and identify which ones work best for you.

Risk management: Develop a robust risk management plan that aligns with your risk tolerance and financial goals. Establish rules for position sizing, stop-loss orders, and profit-taking to protect your capital and minimise losses.

Record and review: Keep a trading journal to record your trades, thoughts, and emotions. Regularly review your journal to identify patterns, mistakes, and areas for improvement. Use this information to refine your trading style and strategies.

Continual learning and adaptation: Stay up-to-date with market news, trends, and developments. Continuously educate yourself on trading techniques and tools to improve your skills and adapt your trading style to changing market conditions.

By taking the time to develop your unique trading style, you'll be better equipped to navigate the world of precious metals trading and build a successful career. Remember that your trading style may evolve over time as you gain experience, so be prepared to adapt and refine your approach as needed.

Continuous Learning and Improvement

A successful career in precious metals trading requires a commitment to continuous learning and improvement. Markets evolve, and new information and tools become available, so it's essential to stay informed and adaptable. Here are some tips for ensuring you continue to learn and improve as a precious metals trader:

Stay updated on market news: Keep an eye on news and developments related to precious metals, such as changes in supply and demand, economic indicators, geopolitical events, and central bank policies. Staying informed will help you make better trading decisions and anticipate market trends.

Follow industry experts: Identify and follow experts and influencers in the precious metals trading community. Read their articles, watch their videos, and listen to their podcasts to gain insights into their strategies, techniques, and market outlooks.

Attend webinars, workshops, and conferences: Participate in educational events to learn from industry professionals and network with other traders. These events can provide valuable insights into new trading strategies, market trends, and technological advancements.

Take online books: Enrol in online books or training programs to deepen your knowledge of precious metals trading and learn new skills. Many educational platforms offer free or affordable books covering a wide range of trading topics.

Read books and research papers: Read books on trading, technical analysis, and fundamental analysis to broaden your understanding of different trading concepts and methodologies. Additionally, research papers can provide in-depth knowledge on specific topics or trading strategies.

Analyse your trading performance: Regularly review your trading journal and performance metrics to identify patterns, strengths, weaknesses, and areas for improvement. Use this information to refine your trading strategies and make adjustments as needed.

Learn from your mistakes: Embrace your mistakes as opportunities for growth and learning. Analyse the factors that contributed to your trading errors, and develop strategies to avoid repeating them in the future.

Join trading communities: Participate in online forums, discussion groups, and social media communities related to precious metals trading. Engaging with other traders can expose you to new ideas, strategies, and perspectives, helping you learn and grow as a trader.

Be open to change: Recognize that markets are dynamic, and your trading style and strategies may need to evolve to stay successful. Be open to adapting your approach as market conditions change or as you learn new information.

Networking and Professional Development

In the world of precious metals trading, networking and professional development are crucial for building a successful career. Connecting with other traders, industry professionals, and experts can provide valuable insights, support, and opportunities for growth. Here are some tips for enhancing your networking and professional development efforts:

Join online communities: Participate in online forums, discussion groups, and social media platforms dedicated to precious metals trading. These communities provide opportunities to share experiences, ask questions, and learn from others in the field.

Attend industry events: Attend conferences, workshops, and seminars focused on precious metals trading, finance, and investing. These events provide opportunities to learn from industry experts, stay up-to-date on market trends, and connect with other traders.

Participate in local meetups: Look for local trading meetups or investment clubs in your area. These groups often hold regular meetings or events where you can meet and network with fellow traders and professionals.

Build relationships with mentors: Identify experienced traders or industry professionals who can serve as mentors or advisors. These individuals can provide valuable guidance, feedback, and insights to help you navigate your trading career.

Engage in social networking: Utilise social media platforms such as LinkedIn, Twitter, and Facebook to connect with other traders, industry professionals, and influencers. Engage in discussions, share your insights, and learn from others in your network.

Offer your expertise: Share your knowledge and experience by writing articles, giving presentations, or hosting webinars on precious metals trading topics. This not only helps you solidify your understanding but also establishes you as an authority in the field.

Continue your education: Pursue relevant certifications or advanced degrees in finance, economics, or related fields to enhance your knowledge and credibility. This can also open doors for networking and professional opportunities.

Join professional associations: Become a member of professional associations or organisations related to precious metals trading or the broader financial industry. These organisations often offer networking events, educational resources, and opportunities for professional growth.

Collaborate on projects: Seek out opportunities to collaborate with other traders or industry professionals on projects, research, or initiatives. Working together can help you build strong relationships and develop new skills.

Maintain your network: Stay in touch with your network and actively nurture your relationships. Regularly reach out to your contacts, offer support, and share relevant information or opportunities.

Balancing Trading with Personal and Professional Life

Successfully trading precious metals requires dedication and focus, but it's also essential to maintain a healthy balance between your trading career and other aspects of your life. Here are some tips to help you strike the right balance between trading and your personal and professional life:

Set boundaries: Establish clear boundaries between your trading activities and personal and professional responsibilities. Allocate specific hours for trading and stick to this schedule. Avoid letting trading interfere with your work or personal life.

Prioritise time management: Use effective time management techniques to make the most of your trading hours while ensuring you have ample time for other commitments. Create a daily routine that includes time for work, trading, family, and leisure activities.

Establish goals: Set realistic and achievable goals for your trading career, personal life, and professional development. Regularly evaluate your progress and make adjustments as needed to maintain a balanced approach to life.

Manage stress: Trading can be stressful, so it's essential to develop healthy coping mechanisms to manage stress. Exercise regularly, practice mindfulness, or engage in relaxation techniques, such as deep breathing or meditation, to keep stress levels in check.
Develop a support network: Cultivate a strong support network of family, friends, and fellow traders who understand the challenges of trading and can offer encouragement, advice, and emotional support.

Take breaks: Give yourself regular breaks from trading to prevent burnout and maintain mental clarity. Schedule vacations or days off to recharge and enjoy other aspects of your life.

Pursue hobbies and interests: Engage in hobbies, sports, or other activities that you enjoy and provide an outlet for relaxation and stress relief. These activities can help you maintain a sense of balance and well-being outside of trading.

Focus on personal growth: Continue to invest in your personal growth and development by pursuing interests, learning new skills, or engaging in self-improvement activities that extend beyond your trading career.

Maintain a healthy lifestyle: Prioritise your physical and mental health by eating well, getting enough sleep, and staying active. A healthy lifestyle supports better decision-making and overall performance in your trading career.

Seek professional help if needed: If you're struggling to balance your trading career with your personal and professional life, consider seeking help from a therapist, counsellor, or life coach who can offer guidance and support.

Conclusion

As we wrap up this extensive and detailed book on precious metals trading, it is vital to revisit the wealth of information we have covered, which will serve as a solid foundation for your journey in this exciting market. We began by introducing the fascinating realm of precious metals, exploring their unique properties, historical significance, and the intrinsic value they hold as both commodities and investments. We delved into the critical role they play in the global economy, including their wide-ranging industrial applications, their appeal during times of economic uncertainty, and their ability to act as a hedge against inflation and currency devaluation.

During our exploration of the four primary precious metals - gold, silver, platinum, and palladium - we examined their distinct properties, applications, and market dynamics, providing valuable insights into what sets each metal apart and their significance in various industries. We also analysed the structure and functioning of the precious metals market, discussing the roles of different market participants, the process of price discovery, and the various market segments, such as physical, derivatives, and exchange-traded products.

Throughout the book, we covered the fundamentals of trading precious metals, including the intricacies of spot, futures, and options markets. We provided an overview of the various trading platforms and brokers available to traders, delving into the key factors to consider when selecting a suitable platform or broker. We discussed order types and execution strategies, helping you understand the mechanics of placing and managing trades effectively. Additionally, we explained the concepts of leverage and margin, highlighting the potential risks and rewards associated with their use. Finally, we clarified the principles of bid and ask prices, ensuring you can make informed decisions when entering or exiting trades.

To better equip you for understanding the forces driving the precious metals market, we delved into the factors that influence precious metals prices, such as supply and demand dynamics, economic indicators, geopolitical events, central bank policies, currency fluctuations, and investment demand. We provided you with a comprehensive overview of both technical and fundamental analysis, discussing chart patterns, indicators, trend identification, support and resistance levels, macro and micro economic factors, industry trends, financial statement analysis, and valuation models.

As you embark on your journey in precious metals trading, remember that success requires a combination of knowledge, skill, discipline, and a commitment to continuous learning and improvement. Stay informed about market developments, adapt your strategies to changing market conditions, and maintain a healthy balance between your trading career and other aspects of your life. By applying the principles and strategies outlined in this comprehensive book, you'll be well-equipped to build a successful and rewarding career in precious metals trading, making the most of the opportunities that this dynamic and ever-evolving market has to offer.

Authors Note

As we reach the conclusion of this journey into the world of Precious Metals trading, I hope you've found the insights, strategies, and advice shared within these pages both enlightening and practical. My aim has been not only to introduce you to the complexities of trading but also to equip you with the knowledge and tools needed for navigating this dynamic market.

Share Your Experience

If this book has helped you in any way, or if you have suggestions for how it could be improved for future readers, I warmly encourage you to leave a review on Amazon. Your feedback is not only invaluable to me as an author but also helps other potential readers make informed decisions. Sharing your experience, thoughts, and the impact this book has had on your trading journey can make a significant difference.

Continue Your Learning Journey

The world of trading is vast, with endless opportunities for growth, learning, and exploration. If you're keen to delve deeper into trading strategies, market analysis, or other financial instruments, I invite you to explore my other books. Each one is crafted to address different facets of the financial markets, offering insights and guidance to enhance your understanding and skills.

You can find my complete collection of works by visiting my Author profile on Amazon. [Link to the author's profile will be provided here]

Whether you're looking to refine your approach to CFD trading, explore new markets, or deepen your understanding of financial analysis, there's a resource for you. My books cover a range of topics designed to support traders and investors at every stage of their journey, from beginners to more experienced market participants.

Final Words

Remember, success in trading is a marathon, not a sprint. It requires patience, discipline, and a commitment to continuous learning and improvement. The financial markets are always evolving, and so should your knowledge and strategies. I wish you the best of luck on your trading journey and hope to accompany you through my writings as you navigate the path to success.

Thank you for choosing this book.